Poetry

Seed Sower, Hat Thrower

Poems about Weather

by Laura Purdie Salas

Capstone
press
Mankato, Minnesota

I Am Fog

I gulp headlights

blanket bridges

seep under your skin

until slices of sun

sizzle me away

Thirsty

Tree leans — a bony hand
over parched and dusty land
Ground cracks like ancient skin,
wrinkles spreading, dark and thin
Arid lands, severe and bleak,
thirst for rushing, bubbling creek

5

Main Street

River road

rises

River road

flows

Hop a boat —

follow

where

River road

goes

Oh!

It rained a few minutes ago

Then winter took over the show

The temperature dropped

The raining soon stopped

And the droplets switched quickly to snow!

Through a windowpane
Streaked with sliding rain
Outside world has changed:
Blurry, velvet stain

Every house and car —
Soft where edges are…
Waterpainting sky
makes each light a star

Softer

Dark and Light

storm

raindrops, misty

falling, gathering, hanging

clouds, fading, sunlight, appearing

bouncing, reflecting, arcing

sparkle, colors

rainbow

Winter Blooms

branches

blooming with ice,

paint a shocking picture

of frosty white trees on winter's

blue sky

13

Wind Is An...

Expert blower

Seed sower

Sailboat go-er

Hat thrower

And, best of all, a

Kite tow-er

Quick!

Lick!

Quick!

Don't drip!

Your sugary,

icy treats on sticks

make your lips

pink and slick

but the searing sun

has a wicked trick

It shimmers 'til

popsicles melt and slip

so take my tip and

Quick!

Lick!

17

18

Bolt

Silver flash dances

    from sky to earth in one leap —

Electrifying!

Wild Wind

Rushing wind

Roaring wind

Whirling, twirling

Warring wind

Ripping wind

Whipping wind

Please release your

Gripping wind

Nearing wind

Clearing wind

Finally,

Disappearing wind

21

Clouds

Vanilla cotton candy

Pillows meant for kings

Fluffy bunny rabbits

Enormous seagull wings

I check the sky at recess

To see what each day brings

I never dreamed that clouds could make

So many different things!

23

24

No More Leaves

Icy

Cold

Icy

Clear

Lonely

Elm tree's frozen tear

Ice Writers

New-ice   Gliding

Colliding,

Skating a glossy, frozen lake

Silver-blade   Writing

Look at the lines and shapes we make

Striding,

Sliding

Guiding,

The Language of Poetry

Alliteration — to have the same beginning sound for several words

Repetition — the use of a word or phrase more than one time

Rhyme — to have an end sound that is the same as the end sound of another word

Rhythm — the pattern of beats in a poem

Acrostic

The subject of the poem is written straight down the page. Each line of the poem starts with a letter from the word. "No More Leaves" (page 25) is an acrostic poem.

Cinquain

A poem with five lines. The first line has two syllables. The second line has four, the third has six, the fourth has eight, and the last line has two syllables. "Winter Blooms" (page 12) is an example of a cinquain.

Free Verse

A poem that does not follow a set pattern or rhythm. It often does not rhyme. "I Am Fog" (page 3) is an example of free verse.

Haiku

A short poem that describes a scene in nature. It has five syllables in the first line, seven syllables in the second line, and five syllables in the third line. "Bolt" (page 19) is a haiku.

Limerick

A five-line poem that follows a certain rhythm. The first, second, and fifth lines rhyme, and so do the third and fourth lines. "Oh!" (page 9) is an example of a limerick.

Glossary

ancient (AYN-shuhnt) — very old

arc (ARK) — a curved line, like a rainbow

arid (AIR-id) — dry

bleak (BLEEK) — empty and sad

blurry (BLUR-ee) — smeared or unclear

collide (kuh-LIDE) — to crash together

electrify (i-LEK-truh-fye) — to shock and excite

parched (PARCHD) — very thirsty

sear (SEER) — to burn

seep (SEEP) — to flow slowly

severe (suh-VEER) — harsh

shimmer (SHIM-ur) — to shine or sparkle

sow (SOH) — to scatter seeds over the ground so they will grow

stride (STRIDE) — to move forward with long steps

velvet (VEL-vit) — smooth, plush, and soft

Read More

Esbensen, Barbara Juster. *Swing around the Sun: Poems.* Minneapolis: Carolrhoda Books, 2003.

Frank, John. *A Chill in the Air: Nature Poems for Fall and Winter.* New York: Simon & Schuster Books for Young Readers, 2003.

Internet Sites

Facthound offers a safe, fun way to find Internet sites related to this book. All of the sites on FactHound have been researched by our staff.

Here's how:

1. Visit *www.facthound.com*

2. Choose your grade level.

3. Type in this book ID **1429612096** for age-appropriate sites. You may also browse subjects by clicking on letters, or by clicking on pictures and words.

4. Click on the **Fetch It** button.

FactHound will fetch the best sites for you!

Index of Poems

32

A+ Books are published by Capstone Press,
151 Good Counsel Drive, P.O. Box 669, Mankato, Minnesota 56002.
www.capstonepress.com

1 2 3 4 5 6 13 12 11 10 09 08

Library of Congress Cataloging-in-Publication Data
Salas, Laura Purdie.
 Seed sower, hat thrower: Poems about weather/by Laura Purdie Salas.
 p. cm. — (A+ books. Poetry)
 Includes bibliographical references and index.
 Summary: "A collection of original, weather-themed poetry for children accompanied by striking photos. The book demonstrates a variety of common poetic forms and defines poetic devices" — Provided by publisher.
 ISBN-13: 978-1-4296-1209-8 (hardcover)
 ISBN-10: 1-4296-1209-6 (hardcover)
 1. Weather — Juvenile poetry. 2. Children's poetry, American.
I. Title. II. Series.
PS3619.A4256S44 2008
811'.6 — dc22   2007034885

Credits
Jenny Marks, editor; Ted Williams, designer; Scott Thoms, photo researcher

Photo Credits
Bruce Coleman Inc./Gene & Karen Rhoden, 21; Kjell Sandved, 24
Getty Images Inc./Nordic Photos/Kristjan Maack, 26–27; Stone/HMS Group/ Doug McKay, 7; Taxi/Walter Bibikow, 4
iStockphoto/Karyn Kudrna, 10
Shutterstock/Andrew Park, 12–13; David Currier, 18–19; Kivrins Anatolijs, cover, 1, 28; Lee Prince, 22–23; Mark Bond, 14; mypokcik, 8–9; paulaphoto, 17; Pichugin Dmitry, 11; Thomas Hruschka, 2–3

Note to Parents, Teachers, and Librarians
Seed Sower, Hat Thrower: Poems about Weather uses colorful photographs and a nonfiction format to introduce children to poetry while building knowledge of weather. This book is designed to be read independently by an early reader or to be read aloud to a pre-reader. The images help early readers and listeners understand the poems and concepts discussed. The book encourages further learning by including the following sections: The Language of Poetry, Glossary, Read More, Internet Sites, and Index. Early readers may need assistance using these features.